AFTER THE SOLSTICE

AFTER THE SOLSTICE

POEMS BY FRED DINGS

ORCHISES   WASHINGTON   1993

Copyright © 1993 Fred Dings

Library of Congress Cataloging in Publication Data

Dings, Fred, 1952-
After the solstice : poems / by Fred Dings.
p. cm.
ISBN 0-914061-34-8 : $12.95
I. Title.
PS3554.I49A69   1993
    811'.54--dc20   93-18470
                                                CIP

Poems included in this collection originally appeared in the following journals:

ANTIOCH REVIEW   "Odysseus on the Côte d'Azur"
BLOOMSBURY REVIEW   "Paper Bridge"
CAROLINA QUARTERLY   "Swallows at a Quarry Lake"
CONTEXT SOUTH   "The Concession"
DENVER QUARTERLY   "After the Solstice"
HIGH PLAINS LITERARY REVIEW   "At a Cemetery in the Smoky
    Mountains"
IRONWOOD   "Padre Island"
THE MIDNIGHT LAMP   "Waterberries"
THE NEW REPUBLIC   "Redwing Blackbirds" "Sycamores"
    "Riva Looking Towards Sirmione" "Matthew 6: 9-13"
THE NEW YORKER   "Late Marsh"
POET LORE   "Old Men Fishing" "The Pianist as Piano Player"
POETRY NORTHWEST   "Blackbirds Flocked in Evergreens"
SHENANDOAH   "Crabbing"
SOUTH FLORIDA POETRY REVIEW   "One Reason For This"

COVER: Maria Marin

Manufactured in the United States of America
Published by Orchises Press
P. O. Box 20602
Alexandria
Virginia
22320-1602

G6E4C2A

for Maria

CONTENTS

I

Redwing Blackbirds 13
The Machines of Intention 14
Sycamores 15
Aspen Grove in Autumn Snow 16
Autumn Pilgrimage 17
At the Coliseum in Verona 18
Riva Looking Towards Sirmione 19
Waterberries 20
No Shallow Mercy 21
Blackbirds Flocked in Evergreens 22
Swallows at a Quarry Lake 23
Diptych:
I. A Last Request 24
II. Matthew 6: 9-13 25
The Poetry Stone 26

II

Odysseus on the Côte d'Azur 29
At a Cemetery in the Smoky Mountains 30
Waiting in Ashland, Pennsylvania 31
Old Men Fishing 32

The Pine Ridge   33
The Concession   34
A Separate Way   35
Marseilles   36
Narcissus by the Lake   37
Paper Bridge   38

III

One Reason for This   41
After the Solstice   43
Coda: The Body of Light   45
The Spirit of Place   46

IV

The Pianist as Piano Player   49
Stravinsky:
I. Cimiteri San Michele, Venezia   50
II. Chautauqua Park, Boulder, Co   51
Primal Sun, Primal Moon   52
A Point of Will   54
The Potter   55
The Chinese Porcelain Vase   56

V

Herons   59
Crabbing   60
Padre Island   62
Late Marsh   63

Werk des Gesichts ist getan,
tue nun Herz-Werk
an den Bildern in dir, jenen gefangenen
       —RILKE, *Wendung*

I

Redwing Blackbirds

This morning they came like the dying
reclaiming their old lives, delirious
with joy right on the seam of Spring,
streaming in by the tattered thousands
like black leaves blowing back onto the trees.

But the homeless know what's expected by now,
and when the farmer fired into their body,
they rose all around me like trembling
black wounds gaping red at the shoulders,
a river of pain draining into the sky.

Tonight, as I look at the cold sky
and its flock of blue-white scars,
I can't yet turn from Orion's red star
whose trembling red light has travelled for years
to die now into any eyes that will hold it.

The Machines of Intention

Who hasn't at least once walked again
in the rain as a child, stepped back inside

the outside, lured by the drapes of rain,
the dark clusters of glistening trees;

who hasn't once stopped and felt momentarily
alien to the cars below, headlights on, charging

the flooded intersections at cross purposes,
again and again, the machines of intention

half-disappearing in sudden parabolas of froth
at the convened wholeness of the world?

Sycamores

As a child I was enchanted by their white branches,
their cool lightning veining dark woods along streams,
but soon was disappointed they were not *pure* white
and here and there were blotched gray-green.
I see them in a different light now, here in Assisi,

the sun splashing everywhere, swallows sickling the air,
as a girl unshutters her window and waters the geraniums
you see flaming the sills eternally in Italy.
While one arm pours and the other tends the soil,
her skin is clearly unmarred as it brindles

with the olive shadows of the rich green leaves.
Perhaps the blotches of death we so fear when they appear
in the light of age are really the harmless shadows
of something our whole lives have been carefully tending,
something unseen perhaps, but vitally green.

Aspen Grove in Autumn Snow

Above treeline, the mountain is streaked
gray-white by snowfall fallen this year
before even half the leaves, which lie like green
and yellow coins on a white blanket. In an aspen
grove, I am amazed at the sun-glitter trembling
against a western-blue sky and the snow's sequined
surface pocked by leaves warm enough even in death
to melt drills of air through the white powder.
Light is slanting in late afternoon to an amber music,
an intermittent music, like the hiss of trains at a station,
the leaf-whispers rushing as the breeze picks up,
rushing again like surf, like something else
just thought of to say, so many goodbyes
repeated, so many reassurances
before the long parting.

Autumn Pilgrimage

Palettes of autumn leaves, no longer contending for light,
merge among the spruce brush-tips on the far canyonside
like blossoms of slow starvation among the eternally green.

Here, beneath a locust tree's yellow feathers
flying into winter, trail rocks and roots
congeal with deer's blood needled with hairs
dislodged like bristles from a dragged body's brush.

Each night the cold air drags the dying year
down over the leaves, thinning off more green
until these Indian-summer days leaf-people are drawn
at last into the world's cathedral falling in stained tatters,
their sighs of wonder stippling the eternal air
as the tracks of death lead them on into the canyon
like lovers enthralled late in life with the kindred
hues of experience dragged into each other's face,
homing deeper and deeper into one another's hills.

At the Coliseum in Verona

From the coliseum tonight in the Piazza Bra,
the sounds of *Aida* soar towards the stars
more tenderly than when our stadiums roar
for sudden pop flies that rise
like high white notes out of sight.
The cut grass bleeds its fragrance in the air.
On stone bench rings, the audience sits transfixed
all the way up to the stone bowl's lip
where the music wells over in widening rings
into a darkness and out to a silence that even
the lungs of Pavarotti cannot reach.
However much I might wish otherwise, I'm afraid
the stars are not the eyes of some dark audience
that peers down on our lives, and there well may be
no sovereign ear pressed against our atmosphere.
I'm here inside this bag of skin no less
than tortured animals and Christians were
two thousand years ago when they performed
their last acts for bored Romans. Perhaps
it's only we who ever listen. Perhaps
it's only we who can.

Riva Looking Towards Sirmione

At the stem end of the great blue pear of Lake Garda
between Alps where the rain has just slashed,
a rainbow arcs among the clouds' blue rocks.
Lake water trembles between stone shoulders,
the same color as the storm-ashened sky.
Haze hovers there like a white fence,
between the heavy gun-metal blue water
and the sculpted blue vapors in high winds.
The algae on the boatdock steps underwater
are no less green than the trees on the mountains.
Rain pocks the body of the lake into thin skins of water
which reflect for a moment, then are gone.

Waterberries

Rain-choked earthworms stretched on roads
like pieces of broken rivers flowing nowhere.
I was mourning you among the soaked and leafless woods,
trying to lift a little the way mist was lifting
from the ground, wrapping faint gauze around dark limbs,
trying to focus on the timelessness of stones.

Though the pain could not be willed away,
a quietness came that let me see
shining among the nets of branches
waterberries formed on twig ends in the rain.
I came close in that lonely place, as you would have,
and saw in the miniature globes reflections
of the world around them, upside down,
more than the premonitions of promised fruit.

No Shallow Mercy

In the lake cove beneath an overhanging wind-combed locust,
spatters of yellow leaves float on an interlude of water
like the pollen of old age making its last long love
to the consummate earth, pressing lightly towards center
on the narrow plain where air and water separate
as a matter of weight. They sort apart and sift siltward
or drift on ribswells of water sighing rimward, yellowing
the shore like sleepcrust on a dream-journeyed eye.

But then from deeper water a swarm of ashen minnows
streams into the lakelobe's shallows as if locust leaves
turned chameleon and convened in that darker world,
swirling like marionette filings beneath an invisible magnet,
charting like lines on a topo map a perfect mime of the doorless
water's edge, coralled for the undeniable large fish
cleaving forward like sudden thickenings of water
ripping through their body until the surface boils
with a rain-spatter of white bellies leapt quivering
from their element. After each charge, the minnows re-swarm,
searching the edge, finding no shallow mercy.

Blackbirds Flocked in Evergreens

These blackbirds have nothing
to do with the music
building where
some practice the luxury
of 20th century atonality.

They have flocked this night
in these evergreens, trying
only to keep warm, finding
Iowa springs don't come easy.

I make them uneasy
coming up in the dark.
They look like the night sky
fracturing among branches
and won't piece together
until I leave.

To hell with Arnold Schönberg.
I'm soon going

to find a cold pine branch
and wrap my feet around it,
I don't care who comes,
I won't let go.

Swallows at a Quarry Lake

Though it might have been better never
to have dipped so deeply for our needs,
the earth is answering with the patience of water
as from a stone ledge on a cliff's face
a mother swallow teaches her child
how to feed on insects from the water's surface
while each time the young one dives too harshly
and splashes down, destroying the water's clear vision.
So he is called back to the stone
ledge to watch as she falls freely,
then banks and turns and follows
the elegant scythe of her wings
to just bring her mouth to its need,
stitching lightly across the surface,
leaving delicate rings widening and wedding
on the fragile threshold of the air.

Diptych

I. A Last Request

When night comes with his censer, strewing smoke,
and the road darkens, the road I love most because it leads
nowhere, I want enough time to remember a few small kindnesses
given freely and the way you looked one summer evening long ago,
I want enough time to touch the whole rosary of moments I have lived by,
so that, when my life exhales from my body, it may be with a fullness
that is whispered like a carefully gathered prayer into the ear of time.

II. Matthew 6: 9-13

Blue herons that fish in silence,
webs that sag with dew,
old pines in mist,
the snow at sea,
and hues as they merge in evening,
rain on mossed rocks,
and crackling flames,
and a breeze touched with brine,
and leaf-stained light in autumn,
Gandhi, Bach, Monet, Maria,
and a stream pool laved with pollen,
the surf as it lathers
and then hisses on the beaches,
the twilight, the stillness

        :these things

The Poetry Stone

An empty shinto altar burns invisibly with time.
A footbridge arcs the still blue pond in early morning mist,
and willows dip their leafless yellow hair along the edge
where gold and blood-red speckled koi drift silently beneath
the cobalt-glazed reflection like underwater sunsets.
The empty furrows of raked white sand in meditation plots
stand ready to receive all thought, the way the winding path
of jigsaw slate receives the pink azaleas as they fall,
and standing like a gateway to this place, a trellis of wisteria
hangs its clustered purple blossoms down like grapes
already filled with memory's wine. Not far from these
it stands, the poetry stone, among the broadleaved evergreens
and pines, its smooth unpolished marble face, gray-rose,
still wet from rain, inscribed with lines which say,

"Here I found that self-same spring
                        I once had long ago."

II

Odysseus on the Côte d'Azur

Kalypso's hotel, with its sunburned tiles
and calcium stucco walls, lulls as always
in the evening shade of palms whose fountains
of fronds toss lightly as tousled feathers.

But it's an old show.

Here by the water beached rocks wash
their languid green hair and pin-like stars
glitter everywhere on the surface,
pierce the eyes and then vanish,
getting nowhere.

                Even home is an ending
when the odyssey won't end in our hearts
and something happens or doesn't to leave
our lives weeping on the edge of things.

Even here trees strain toward sunset
on the ends of long black chains,
for we would follow the light forever,
if we could, homeward, where the sun sails
its fiery billow over the deepening blue.

At a Cemetery in the Smoky Mountains

This morning wind and rain broke white bloodroot
petals from their yellow coronets
and scattered them like swollen stars
onto the poor red soil. Now clouds
shroud the peaks, and potholes, rain-filled,
shine like jigsaw pieces of sky.

These hill people died at tasks
I barely even know, so why am I here
where a lost river was cut more or less
into six-foot lengths and laid out under stones?

Do we weight their heads with these tags
the moss and rain are trying to erase
to hold them
down or lid their bones
from strange teeth like the present
homing on femoral blue haze
seeping from that deep hole of the past?
Days are lost this way. Lives.

Here, a young girl, mired, could not wedge
more than one year into time.
And what are we to do?
We have arranged these stones in rows like teeth
that have nothing but the air to cut
against. At each stands a sentinel
of plastic flowers provided by the State.
A swallowtail butterfly lifts among them
on barred yellow wings,
finding each time
only a little scum of rain.

Waiting in Ashland, Pennsylvania

(for James Wright)

Spring rains have salved away
the coal-dusted scab of snow,
but the trees' new teeth are already yellow and weak
and sooty clapboard houses still fester on the hills.

Each day the men climb away from the sun
down the splinter of air they've carved
in the mountainside, mining a black vein in the earth.

Now and then the vein will collapse,
and women will end sipping amnesia in tombs
while hammers chisel to thieve their venous dark.

Some are so lonely they will accept.

But most would rather hold the night home
huddled between their own arms,
yearning for a salve of warm words,
silent and frightened as secrets
that have lost their voice.

Old Men Fishing

In the afternoon they sit like iguanas
on the rocks, their leathery throats
evolving into wordlessness
as they interrogate the river's current
with their hooks. The sun burns, a huge
shadeless bulb whose filament heart
they know to be forked. They barter
with small fry as bait which the current
carves away, leaving curved steel bone
posing the question beneath all flesh.
They wait for an answer, gazing at the cliff-
face mirrored on the water, knowing
it will crack even for small things,
for a root begging darkness or the pure
lodging structure of a little ice.

The Pine Ridge

Tripping on rocks she went up the draw
to that razorback ridge where the topmost pines
bristle and fray against the sky.
She went among that stand of Ponderosas
which in time have claimed the entire hillside
with their scaly bark as dry as cracking flesh
and needles like thirst-clenched leaves.
And on the many layered net of fallen
needles (through which nothing grows)
you'll find discharged cones flared and still
spined though there are no seeds to guard
and perhaps a young doe lying with some comfort
the way a mind might couch
even on painful memories, dried and fallen into patterns,
if it does not turn too roughly upon them.
She stayed there for hours until the sun lowered
away and the pine ridge, as if tired of bright heat,
slowly turned its back—about the time
trees seem to soften and grow fragrant
and the lengthening shadows ease this way like a slow blue river
or the long blending fingers of an uncertain hand.
She came with her head slightly lowered and turned
as if listening to something I could not hear.
She stood for awhile outside her door
before she opened it.

The Concession

Circuit-worn and tired, in a snow-filled forest,
I came to a small clearing
where a trapped beaver humped down against the snow
like a beaten child or dog cowed by his barking master.
I don't know why it came outside
its warm ice-glazed lodge of logs and branches
where one cool glide retrieved all needs
from a cache of tender twigs,
but when I saw his frightened cloudy eyes,
I shuffled slowly closer on my knees
as carefully as one approaches a memory of great injury
and spoke in an assuaging monotone
as gently as a mother might caress.
Its right leg stretched taut as rope
fraying to bone; its whole being strained
opposite forged rings staked at the center
in a circle of worn snow. It seemed
like a darkened moon in endless apogee
or the clubfooted hand of a clock's face
forever measuring the radius and cycle of its time.
I had hoped, with one quick slight of hand,
to snap open the steel jaw
and unsnag its whole body.
But when I reached, its censoring teeth
snapped at my fingers
and would have cut had I been slower.
I raised my foot to crush its skull,
but then thought better
and left the animal to gnaw itself off,
fall pelt or prey,
or freeze in its frozen zero.

A Separate Way

When we allow the world to go its way
like a car roaring down a country road
muffling in the miles, the stunned silence
begins to thaw and small sounds crawl back
in the meadows and marsh, intermittent, all
through the dark, awakening and finding themselves
in the stars blinking overhead . . .

When we allow the world to go its way,
it goes and leaves us alone with the selves
we left behind to begin to understand the years,
the heaviness, and the miracle of our own
inexplicable breaths tugging us forward,
leading us through all the tides of the mind,
closing our lives with the sutures of time . . .

When we allow the world to go its way,
sometimes it won't go and we can hear
in the snow crystals ticking on our pane
the newly dead breaking their bones in the earth,
leaving the still white ash of time,
and the newly alive crowding to our sill,
bringing the blank white page minds of beginning . . .

When we allow the world to go its way
and at last can drift across our own lost seas,
we are restored in time to whole beingness
and flow with the full length of our riverness
into the mouth of the moment,
and then we can say to the world without loss
"I will go now in my own way."

Marseilles

Sewage drains seaward under the streets,
mixing its gray smell with the salt air.
By day she arranges for the evening
(as she always has) her crooked seams
and the blue and rouge cafes which daub
her inner harbor, so that at night her waterfront
glitters like a goblet rimmed with lights,
held in the tips of her dark surrounding streets.
But then with the hours you are drawn away
from the shifting pleasures and the faceless sea,
down the ancient alleys where buildings loom
like clamps. Only then do you find yourself
alone in the stillness, listening to the whisper
of your own breathing as your lungs fill
with the invisible air, depending on something
you can't even see, waiting for you there, always.

Narcissus by the Lake

Clear water cups in the mountain's rock palm,
nursed by rain and runnels from snowpacks
cradled high between crags like clouds
that rested one night, then decided to stay.
Spruce and fir crowd as if coming down
from the barren divide to drink or gaze
into this huge mirror, their dark reflections
eyelashing the rim like stalactites
at the mouth of a deep blue cave.
Trout rise and touch the surface
like teardrops spreading a choir of silent
notes across the reflection of the sky.
When I cup into the mirror of my face,
one more ring widens and weds its voice
to the silent harmonic of the world.

Paper Bridge

Sometimes it seems our lives are the childhoods of stars:
the differences, the severances, the expanding *from*
building to a place in space.

I think of those who hoard their heart's coinage,
tolling the bridges of flesh arcing toward them
or burning them . . .

I think of a comet as part of a star's body
travelling the lonely years, arcing toward another,
a bridge of light like Christ nailing himself to both shores.

I think of you tonight, wherever you are,
high in some glittering constellation. Come down
and stay for awhile, here, on the earth.

III

One Reason for This

Mrs. Cavagna's farm is a brief staircase of terraces
above the valley where the Ticino River, straitjacketed
in concrete, spears straight into Lago di Maggiore.
The few grapevines are trained in rows of wishbones
along wooden trellises and each year raise themselves
on tendrils of child-wood curling question marks
over the dead. A black serpentine of asphalt flows
through her land like a river of grief down to Locarno
and ribbons up along the razoring mountainside to Monti Motti
from where I had just come from drinking cappucino
and stopping to examine in a stone wall on the inside
elbow of a hairpin an empty sleeve of skin
a snake had lodged deliberately in tortuous meanders
among the rocks to push from the center of the old.

A storm was laboring against the mountain,
its breath getting colder and faster, its swollen
blue body threatening to unseam, and she
was hurrying to save from rain-rot the hay
that her wintering goats would transform into milk.
She was glad to see me, her new neighbor,
and smiled with a winter face that has seen the wind
and carries its bootprint as do snowdrifts and dunes
and welcomed me with her hands so hardened in layers
from years of guiding the scythe's moon-sliver of steel
past her feet that even if one of the butterflies
winking from the unmown tatters at the field's edge
would have at last come and landed in her palm
she would have seen it, but not felt it.
As I worked to help her, her vertebrae screamed
to unpile until she locked in a grimace
and was forced to the house, the unpaned windows
flaming with geraniums, the stones straining at the mortar
like lost children the mountain was calling back home.

So I stood alone on that Ticino mountainside,
wrapped in wind beneath a lowering blue palm,
raking the earth-hair in mounds the wind
wanted to unpile, as did generations before me,
the hard whip of necessity cracking the cadence
of their lives. And I thought how so many now,
less bound but not more free, tired and afraid,
duplicate their days in a long diminuendo of the past
they call the present, sleepwalking through the miracle
of slow death, settling like a stylus in the most indirect
spiral inward they can find, breaking off and repeating
at the grooveless land around the totem of the world.

I let the rake-teeth settle among the stubble,
caressing the unexplored center beneath my feet,
wondering how long Mrs. Cavagna could go on
like the farm's one leg since her husband died,
each autumn staining her bare feet into burgundy boots,
marching the blood out of the grapes into the bottles
laid in the stonewalled cellar in rows like emerald
ships sailing into time until the day the blood becomes wine,
becomes spirit, and flows through the mouth into clearer glass,
into another mouth, another body, down
through the layers of pain to places still so tender
even the gentle fingers of the burgundy bring tears
streaming like run-off from the thawing soul.
That is how I found her with her bare table
and empty glass when I came like a clubfoot
eclipsing her doorway in from the rain,
not close enough to come any closer
as she strained to hide her embarassment.
So not knowing what to do, I said
goodbye as kindly as I could and walked out,
drenching in the run-off from the sky.

After the Solstice

I was in the albergo on Via Mazzanti,
a capillary cobbled street where tired blood
can begin on its way back to the heart,
when he splashed against me in the lobby,
a brass band named Tony from New York,
his autobiography riding on waves of whiskey
breath like the Venus of self-love.
Every year for forty-six years since he chased
the Germans like vermin through these streets
and held a local girl, briefly, in marriage,
he has boomeranged back here, snagged
on the past, baiting the hook
of loneliness with excessive friendliness
in vain against the speechless bodies
riddled with time and the face of a girl
slipping around the corners out of sight.
Then when his desperation implodes,
he bunkers in his room for days,
eyes branching into the red forests
of sleeplessness and the cheap nepenthe
he sucks down, crawling to that last white
door to forgetfulness, the hospital bed.

What I say to him now I say
to myself because I'm not sure
how we can live
past the summer's solstice of our lives,
free from the backward suck of loss,
when each day the sun shatters into stars
and the entire moon of human hope
seems a white tick bloating
on the merely-speculated hide of the dark.

As I sit here where my father used to sit
along the Adige, Verona clinging to its curves
like a child to its mother's hips, I
wish I knew how this ancient vein
keeps stepping into its body,
every moment, generation after generation,
without worrying if all that waits is
that coffin of rivers, the heart of water, the sea.

Yet, on certain days I seem to see
a little more with less
like a pupil widening in the dark,
and I wonder now if the high-water mark
of light, the whole brass band of experience,
was to get our utter attention
on the face of this world, the present
tense of being, to follow its long diminuendo
to its dark and lonely center, our senses
refining as we wean from the mother of light
and abandon ourselves to the dark and shine.

Coda: The Body of Light

Each night at this time
when the sky bleeds into gauze
and pines darken around invisible deer
and air enters and embraces everything I see,

the sun's cells unswarm loosely into stars,
stretching into and around the darkness,
though the rim-quenched eye is lost
and Reverence unclasps its hands.

The Spirit of Place

Winter's last remnants now thin to white muslin
on the distant blue cones still peaked in snow.
A plane drones overhead while a steady spring warmth
irons nerves to a calmness we thought would never come.
New leaves cluster like small green fountains spurting
everywhere from the trees. A slow breeze moves among them
in long whispers like the soft abrasions of air we speak.
The birds outside our five open windows built their nests
last week, their tweezer beaks arriving each time with a pinch
of what will do. Now they persuade intruders away with song,
and white globes speckled with dark stars lie gathered
in the secret woven palms of grass and string.
With so much future present, our winter's passport
longings for Tuscan hills and golden foreign light
seem to have drifted away with the clouds.
Today it seems our best days could be lived anywhere,
maybe, now, even here.

IV

The Pianist as Piano Player

Every little hollow in time, he sits
on the bench before the black hearth with
his blueprints for feeling, his programmed weather.
Tone arms settle onto the yin and yang keys,
playing circles around the same pieces: the mountains,
the trenches, the storms, the ritual baths of harmony.
His marionette fingers build the same marvelous dwellings
in the air, those wombs his heart retreats to
each evening like a cow's udder to be eased.
And tension leaks from his twitching hands,
and finger-roots suck confidence and life from the composed
until the turtle spirit begins to ease out of its shell
and its stubby legs struggle to touch ground,
the drawbridge lowering and head periscoping into the world
as if charmed out of its basket by the distant music
of love and pain so far, far away.

Stravinsky

I. Cimiteri San Michele, Venezia

The waterbus ferried us to the island's stone gate,
cypresses rose behind walls like black flames,
lizards scurried among forests of marble stumps
in lines like regiments marching into time.
In a small alcove near Pound, two white slabs
of marble lay flat like twin doors to the earth—

Igor Stravinsky　　　　　*Vera Stravinsky*

were inlaid in Russian-blue calligraphy,
and a bronze cross was inlaid at Vera's feet,
but Igor's was pried away, leaving a white
hole to gather and form the rain.

II. Chautauqua Park, Boulder, CO

One month later, Russian-blue evening sky
above the foothills' pine-feathered flatirons,
Rite of Spring brassing knives into the air,
timpani throbbing like hearts about to explode,
bows sawing at strands of gut short-circuiting
at the cross they keep trying to make,
then stunned silence
before palms drum applause
on the far side of the earth for this violent birth,
and the orchestra's white tuxedos rise into the air
like doors waiting to open at the next deep breath.

Primal Sun, Primal Moon

In those last days of men's belief,
a god must have seen the sun set for the first time,
felt the ground of understanding shift beneath his feet,
watched the eternal light slip down, impossibly down,
then bloody, spill, impale upon the trees,
turning bruise, then black.

We all have some such primal loss,
something we could not bear but did,
something perhaps we have spent our lives
trying to replace or revise.

Maybe that is why we have made so much
of the moon, so many hymns,
because that first stunned night,
opposite where the sun had just died,
something like the sun's blanched face rose,
ghostlike, shining, rescuing the darkness,
the way a loved one's face
or some invented sun
has since climbed into the nights of our lives.

Memory is like that. Memory *is* moonrise,
both "good" and "bad" (and so is "lunacy"
where the pain is great enough),
and at times when life hurls us downward
or we need to take measure of our lives
and voluntarily climb into the dark,
assenting even if we don't know it to death,
it is the bright wafer we take upon our tongues
in our communion with the night

in order to speak with the light of past days,
saying "I remember, I re-member,"
and so rejoin the dismembered body of our experience
with thought, in a fullness
greater than present time or loss or confusion,
and in the end we may,
with a few persons who have labored long
in the fields of memory, not only reflect,
but radiate with the received light of our world.

A Point of Will

"These hayrows look like the hills of giant moles,"
she says, her face reflecting the rose-hued clouds,
the damp air fragrant with cut grass and wild rose.
Set on the hill, a farmhouse window beacons
its gold reflection somewhere into twilight,
out past the last musical whirrings of redwing blackbirds
perched on wooden fence posts webbed with brown wire,
out past the patches of fields diffusing in July haze
whose hedges are so thickly frothed with blossoms
they look like stars about to effervesce
around the pale gold blaze of the rising moon.

Soon the hay will be wired in tight bales
and either left on the field like headstones
or gathered in for wintering cows to sculpt into milk:
which will be a point of will, I suppose,
nursing in the cradle of this evening
where things come to rhyme on parallel planes
by reflection translated and perceived
or by some mutual resolution towards life.

The Potter

(a photograph by Edward Curtis)

Supplicant clay on clay, the ancient potter
kneels on the earth, her moon-silver hair,
leathery skin, and face almost lost in shadow
with years of throwing bowls into being, years of
turning lumps of clay on the wheel and impressing
an absence into the clay's presence to hold
the needed water and kernels of life. She listens
to the at first faint strains of that voice
in the mind's winds and the blood's tides
which begins whispering *give form to the clay*
as God Itself must have first heard it
before turning us on the years of experience
to impress us with what we call loss,
Its invisible hands forming gloves of matter
to fit with the accuracy of love. So it is love
she brings to her bowl-making, making nearly
any unusual shape so long as the bowlness
holds what needs to be held. Her fingers
crumble with drying clay like roots too long
out of the soil they shape and soon will become.
She leans close to the last word of the soil,
over all her bowls and jars with their mouths
through which all that enters must also leave,
and leaves each enclosing a lungful of air
with all the words fallen out of it,
air resting merely inside among itself,
unchanged and unchanging, for a time,
neither drawn in nor pushed away.

The Chinese Porcelain Vase

Framed by the vestibule's glass doors, a few clouds
remember daylight in faint hues. We turn inside
down the stairs, holding the marble balustrades,
our feet settling softly in the concave memories
of many who have come this way, the hollows
worn into stone like cupped palms.
We come to the furthest room
which is small and dark except for one light
above a glass case holding a baluster vase.

Here, this inspired clay released
from some solitude at the brink
of history has come to us miraculously, diked
behind thick panes, safe
from a sea of unmeaning hands,
smooth like the remembering of old hands,
a faithful emerald lung that will not expire
as long as it is faithfully loved.

Two dragons handle its slender neck
as if ascending toward the flared dark mouth
through which all that enters must also leave.
We move closer, and when I tilt my face
to the light above and look along its green horizon,
I see for the first time
transparent herons poised
like reflections floating on the glaze,
fishing among iridescent flowers.

When I move to tell you, they are gone.

But floating on your dark irises
I see my own diminished face.

V

Herons

Not expecting a ripcord for future times
as the sky's rose-blue eggshell darkened
and our green canoe slid like a smooth finger
over a wet painting of the world and cicadas
shivered from the trees which rose
like ancient cities inside walls of reeds,
we nosed into a backwater alcove,
a wild blue note off the main stream,
thinking we were alone, but
gliding right beside the great blue
whose stilts both instantly broke
and gray snake neck recoiled then jabbed
at the empty sky, hauling on huge tattered flaps
into the air like a feathered pterodactyl
crawling back over eons of marsh.
We listened to the "grallk" "grallk" grow fainter
like a rusty hinge on a shrinking door closing forever,
then sat centered in midge-clouds in the after sound
until our breathing dragged us on
and we scuttled from under the wet blanket of night,
spearing towards the next day
and the shooting stars of headlights
like sunfish far away in dark water.

Crabbing

With the land behind us a black rift
between identical shades of blue and
our outboard murmuring its aluminum dream
to ore-laden veins in the earth,
we lift and fall on quiet sighs of water
as it yearns to that center above, the half-moon
like an eye, averted, praying to the East
to lay its naming finger on the world.
We lay our trotline out between buoys—
100 yards of cord stubbed with severed
chicken necks like a crude pearl necklace
offered to the sea, the bloody coil
unravelling behind us from our boat
as something inside us might, snagged
on the world though our breathing dragged us on.
We fasten the other end
and leave time for the enticement of bait,
listening to the green-beige clatter of reeds
that inspired the first musicians
to lash liferafts of panpipes
and give air to their drowning hearts.
We mop our faces and gaze at the seamless weld
of distances we know we will never cross,
trusting the whole sea flows into this finger
of water the way a lover does into his hand
and will give us back at least ourselves
though we come to beg life
from its blood. "Time," my friend says,
and we plow slowly back along the line
which slides like a ridged spine up and over
the plastic-pipe arm clamped to our boatside.

Hooked only on desire, the dreaming sea-spiders follow
to the surface the bitten and sea-blanched necks,
and I web them into this sea too thin for swimming,
dropping them like blue coins into our basket.
At first, as always, there is the clatter of carapace,
of legs skittish above the snapping blue flames,
but soon there reigns an agreement of claws
clamped on claws, on arms, into a face here
and there where lung air bubbles out by an eye.
At first glance they seem joined
in some motionless blue dance, ringed
in a gesture of brotherhood and shared fate
like a universal O of despair. I think
how their basket life seeds a *déjà vu* for tonight
when I will lower them with pincer tongs
into the cauldron, into their last sear of feeling,
and wince, as always, at such drastic love as devouring,
that laying something other against our innermost sides
and absorbing all we can through our walls.
But then, as always, I will smile at such sweet white
meat from such a pinching and bottom-feeding world,
my lips burning with the brine of Old Bay,
then numb with cold beer and distilled spirits on ice.

Padre Island

Meaning "father of solitude,"
it's a long brow of sand like a splinter in the sea
where surf breaks and scrapes at the border
in a wrangle of death, a bier of rotting
gull clumps, cracked crabs, and storm-hewn
forests of kelp rimmed in foam. Inland,
among the nerve-nets of vines, the legions of grass
spears, and prickly pears blistered with buds,
it's an old dialogue of dunes:
those waves of sand so slow whole civilizations
of seaoats surf on them for generations
enduring those others, the senseless white broncos,
saddled only by the wind wisping sand off like steam,
stampeding island life with choking drifts
because they have no roots to bind them.
Days burn with the weight of too much light
like too much pain in service of maturation,
bleaching the colors to a sigh, explaining the land,
convincing fresh water to pull up and drift away
until shade is pared to a few gaunt shapes
and faultlines threading through the grass. But
it's among such remnants the mind must harbor itself:
a lizard clutching an oyster chip,
cooling his face in a crack in the sun;
a meadowlark cresting a man-sized knoll,
playing his liquid flute in the splintering wind.

Late Marsh

We must repeat the lessons of the world
from Ptolemaic to Copernican to after that,
finding Heraclitus with his vanished river gone
though we snag downstream after it, years
later, on the same marsh road, tracking
in the bluish sand of evening the weave
of tire ruts unspooling into the distance,
finding swamped trees in leg irons of ice
and herons stranded in wind-rasped ovals
as the pieces of their vision wave away
and daylight's ruining temple falls
in a pillar of gold scimitars across the water
and fades as the sun's red watch
slips into its pocket, leaving
the bruised sky alone to blacken.